Gone

James H. Schmitz

Alpha Editions

This edition published in 2022

ISBN : 9789356154544

Design and Setting By
Alpha Editions
www.alphaedis.com
Email - info@alphaedis.com

As per information held with us this book is in Public Domain.
This book is a reproduction of an important historical work. Alpha Editions uses the best technology to reproduce historical work in the same manner it was first published to preserve its original nature. Any marks or number seen are left intentionally to preserve its true form.

Contents

GONE FISHING ....- 1 -
  By JAMES H. SCHMITZ ....- 1 -
    THE END OF YEAR ONE ....- 30 -
    THE END OF YEAR TWO ....- 35 -
    THE END OF YEAR FIVE...- 37 -

GONE FISHING

By JAMES H. SCHMITZ

There is no predictable correlation between intelligence and ethics, nor is ruthlessness necessarily an evil thing. And there is nothing like enforced, uninterrupted contemplation to learn to distinguish one from another....

Illustrated by Krenkel

Barney Chard, thirty-seven—financier, entrepreneur, occasional blackmailer, occasional con man, and very competent in all these activities—stood on a rickety wooden lake dock, squinting against the late afternoon sun, and waiting for his current business prospect to give up the pretense of being interested in trying to catch fish.

The prospect, who stood a few yards farther up the dock, rod in one hand, was named Dr. Oliver B. McAllen. He was a retired physicist, though less retired than was generally assumed. A dozen years ago he had rated as one of the country's top men in his line. And, while dressed like an aging tramp in what he had referred to as fishing togs, he was at the moment potentially the country's wealthiest citizen. There was a clandestine invention he'd fathered which he called the McAllen Tube. The Tube was the reason Barney Chard had come to see McAllen.

Gently raising and lowering the fishing rod, and blinking out over the quiet water, Dr. McAllen looked preoccupied with disturbing speculations not connected with his sport. The man had a secrecy bug. The invention, Barney thought, had turned out to be bigger than the inventor. McAllen was afraid of the Tube, and in the forefront of his reflections must be the inescapable fact that the secret of the McAllen Tube could no longer be kept without Barney Chard's co-operation. Barney had evidence of its existence, and didn't really need the evidence. A few hints dropped here and there would have made McAllen's twelve years of elaborate precaution quite meaningless.

Ergo, McAllen must be pondering now, how could one persuade Mr. Chard to remain silent?

But there was a second consideration Barney had planted in the old scientist's mind. Mr. Chard, that knowledgeable man of the world, exuded not at all by chance the impression of great quantities of available cash. His manner, the conservatively tailored business suit, the priceless chip of a platinum watch ... and McAllen needed cash badly. He'd been fairly wealthy himself at one time; but since he had refrained from exploiting the Tube's commercial possibilities, his continuing work with it was exhausting his capital. At least that could be assumed to be the reason for McAllen's impoverishment, which was a matter Barney had established. In months the old man would be living on beans.

Ergo again, McAllen's thoughts must be running, how might one not merely coax Mr. Chard into silence, but actually get him to come through with some much-needed financial support? What inducement, aside from the Tube, could be offered someone in his position?

Barney grinned inwardly as he snapped the end of his cigarette out on the amber-tinted water. The mark always sells himself, and McAllen was well along in the process. Polite silence was all that was necessary at the moment. He lit a fresh cigarette, feeling a mild curiosity about the little lake's location. Wisconsin, Minnesota, Michigan seemed equally probable guesses. What mattered was that half an hour ago McAllen's Tube had brought them both here in a wink of time from his home in California.

Dr. McAllen thoughtfully cleared his throat.

"Ever do any fishing, Mr. Chard?" he asked. After getting over his first shock at Barney's revelations, he'd begun speaking again in the brisk, abrupt manner Barney remembered from the last times he'd heard McAllen's voice.

"No," Barney admitted smiling. "Never quite got around to it."

"Always been too busy, eh?"

"With this and that," Barney agreed.

McAllen cleared his throat again. He was a roly-poly little man; over seventy now but still healthy-looking, with an apple-cheeked, sunburned face. Over a pair of steel-rimmed glasses his faded blue eyes peered musingly at Barney. "Around thirty-five, aren't you?"

"Thirty-seven."

"Married?"

"Divorced."

"Any particular hobbies?"

Barney laughed. "I play a little golf. Not very seriously."

McAllen clicked his tongue. "Well, what do you do for fun?"

"Oh ... I'd say I enjoy almost anything I get involved in." Barney, still smiling, felt a touch of wariness. He'd been expecting questions from McAllen, but not quite this kind.

"Mainly making money, eh? Well," McAllen conceded, "that's not a bad hobby. Practical, too. I ... whup! Just a moment."

The tip of the slender rod in his left hand dipped slightly, and sixty feet out beyond the end of the old dock a green and white bobber began twitching about. Then the bobber suddenly disappeared. McAllen lifted the rod tip a foot or two with a smooth, swift motion, and paused.

"Hooked!" he announced, looking almost childishly pleased.

The fish on the far end of the line didn't seem to put up much of a struggle, but the old man reeled it in slowly and carefully, giving out line from time to time, then taking it back. He seemed completely absorbed. Not until the fish had been worked close to the dock was there a brief minor commotion near the surface. Then McAllen was down on one knee, holding the rod high with one hand, reaching out for his catch with the other. Barney had a glimpse of an unimpressive green and silver disk, reddish froggy eyes. "*Very* nice crappie!" McAllen informed him with a broad smile. "Now—" He placed the rod on the dock, reached down with his other hand. The fish's tail slapped the water; it turned sideways, was gone.

"Lost it!" Barney commented, surprised.

"Huh?" McAllen looked around. "Well, no, young man—I *turned* him loose. He wasn't hooked bad. Crappies have delicate lips, but I use a barbless hook. Gives them better than a fighting chance." He stood up with the rod, dusting the knees of his baggy slacks. "Get all the eating fish I want anyway," he added.

"You really enjoy that sport, don't you?" Barney said curiously.

McAllen advised him with the seriousness of the true devotee to try it some time. "It gets to you. It can get to be a way of living. I've been fishing since I was knee-high. Three years ago I figured I'd become good enough to write a book on the subject. I got more arguments over that book—sounder arguments too, I'd say—than about any paper I've published in physics." He looked at Barney a moment, still seriously, and went on. "I told you wetting a line would calm me down after that upset you gave me. Well, it has—fishing is as good a form of therapy as I know about. Now I've been doing some thinking. I'd be interested ... well, I'd like to talk some more about the Tube with you, Mr. Chard. And perhaps about other things too."

"Very gratifying to hear that, doctor," Barney said gravely. "I did regret having to upset you, you know."

McAllen shrugged. "No harm done. It's given me some ideas. We'll talk right here." He indicated the weather-beaten little cabin on the bank behind Barney. "I'm not entirely sure about the California place. That's one reason I suggested this trip."

"You feel your houseman there mightn't be entirely reliable?"

"Fredericks unreliable? Heavens no! He knows about the Tube, of course, but Fredericks *expects* me to invent things. It wouldn't occur to him to talk to an outsider. He's been with me for almost forty years."

"He was," remarked Barney, "listening in on the early part of our conversation today."

"Well, he'll do that," McAllen agreed. "He's very curious about anyone who comes to see me. But otherwise ... no, it's just that in these days of sophisticated listening devices one shouldn't ever feel too sure of not being overheard."

"True enough." Barney glanced up at the cabin. "What makes you so sure of it here, doctor?"

"No reason why anyone would go to the trouble," McAllen said. "The property isn't in my name. And the nearest neighbor lives across the lake. I never come here except by the Tube so I don't attract any attention."

He led the way along the dock. Barney Chard followed, eyes reflectively on the back of McAllen's sunburned neck and the wisps of unclipped white hair sticking out beneath his beaked fishing cap. Barney had learned to estimate accurately the capacity for physical violence in people he dealt with. He would have offered long odds that neither Dr. McAllen nor Fredericks, the elderly colored man of all work, had the capacity. But Barney's right hand, slid idly into the pocket of his well-tailored coat, was resting on a twenty-five caliber revolver. This was, after all, a very unusual situation. The human factors in themselves were predictable. Human factors were Barney's specialty. But here they were involved with something unknown—the McAllen Tube.

When it was a question of his personal safety, Barney Chard preferred to take no chances at all.

From the top of the worn wooden steps leading up to the cabin, he glanced back at the lake. It occurred to him there should have been at least a suggestion of unreality about that placid body of water, and the sun low and red in the west beyond it. Not that he felt anything of the kind. But less than an hour ago they had been sitting in McAllen's home in Southern California, and beyond the olive-green window shades it had been bright daylight.

"But I can't ... I really can't imagine," Dr. McAllen had just finished bumbling, his round face a study of controlled dismay on the other side of the desk, "whatever could have brought you to these ... these extraordinary conclusions, young man."

Barney had smiled reassuringly, leaning back in his chair. "Well, indirectly, sir, as the pictures indicate, we might say it was your interest in fishing. You see, I happened to notice you on Mallorca last month...."

By itself, the chance encounter on the island had seemed only moderately interesting. Barney was sitting behind the wheel of an ancient automobile, near a private home in which a business negotiation of some consequence was being conducted. The business under discussion happened to be Barney's, but it would have been inexpedient for him to attend the meeting in person. Waiting for his associates to wind up the matter, he was passing time by studying an old man who was fishing from a small boat offshore, a hundred yards or so below the road. After a while the old fellow brought the boat in, appeared a few minutes later along the empty lane carrying his tackle and an apparently empty gunny sack, and trudged unheedingly past the automobile and its occupant. As he went by, Barney had a sudden sense of recognition. Then, in a flash, his mind jumped back twelve years.

Dr. Oliver B. McAllen. Twelve years ago the name had been an important one in McAllen's field; then it was not so much forgotten as deliberately buried. Working under government contract at one of the big universities, McAllen had been suddenly and quietly retired. Barney, who had a financial interest in one of the contracts, had made inquiries; he was likely to be out of money if McAllen had been taken from the job. Eventually he was informed, in strict confidence, that Dr. McAllen had flipped. Under the delusion of having made a discovery of tremendous importance, he had persuaded the authorities to arrange a demonstration. When the demonstration ended in complete failure, McAllen angrily accused some of his most eminent colleagues of having sabotaged his invention, and withdrew from the university. To protect a once great scientist's name, the matter was being hushed up.

So Mallorca was where the addled old physicist had elected to end his days—not a bad choice either, Barney had thought, gazing after the retreating figure. Pleasant island in a beautiful sea—he remembered having heard about McAllen's passion for angling.

A day later, the Mallorca business profitably concluded, Barney flew back to Los Angeles. That evening he entertained a pair of tanned and shapely ladies whose idea of high fun was to drink all night and go deep-sea fishing at dawn. Barney shuddered inwardly at the latter notion, but promised to see the sporting characters to the Sweetwater Beach Municipal Pier in time to catch a party boat, and did so. One of the girls, he noticed not without satisfaction—he had become a little tired of the two before morning—appeared to turn a delicate green as she settled herself into the gently swaying half-day boat beside the wharf. Barney waved them an amiable farewell and was about to go when he noticed a plump old man sitting in the stern of the boat among other anglers, rigging up his tackle. Barney checked sharply, and blinked. He was looking at Oliver B. McAllen again.

It was almost a minute before he felt sure of it this time. Not that it was impossible for McAllen to be sitting in that boat, but it did seem extremely unlikely. McAllen didn't look in the least like a man who could afford nowadays to commute by air between the Mediterranean and California. And Barney felt something else trouble him obscurely as he stared down at the old scientist; a notion of some kind was stirring about in the back corridors of his mind, but refused to be drawn to view just then.

He grew aware of what it was while he watched the party boat head out to sea a few minutes later, smiled at what seemed an impossibly fanciful concoction of his unconscious, and started towards the pier's parking lot. But when he had reached his car, climbed in, turned on the ignition, and lit a cigarette, the notion was still with him and Barney was no longer smiling. Fanciful it was, extremely so. Impossible, in the strict sense, it was not. The longer he played it around, the more he began to wonder whether his notion mightn't hold water after all. If there was anything to it, he had run into one of the biggest deals in history.

Later Barney realized he would still have let the matter drop there if it hadn't been for other things, having nothing to do with Dr. McAllen. He was between operations at present. His time wasn't occupied. Furthermore he'd been aware lately that ordinary operations had begun to feel flat. The kick of putting over a deal, even on some other hard, bright character of his own class, unaccountably was fading. Barney Chard was somewhat frightened because the operator game was the only one he'd ever found interesting; the other role of well-heeled playboy wasn't much more than a manner of killing time. At thirty-seven he was realizing he was bored with life. He didn't like the prospect.

Now here was something which might again provide him with some genuine excitement. It could be simply his imagination working overtime, but it wasn't going to do any harm to find out. Mind humming with pleased though still highly skeptical speculations, Barney went back to the boat station and inquired when the party boat was due to return.

He was waiting for it, well out of sight, as it came chugging up to the wharf some hours later. He had never had anything to do directly with Dr. McAllen, so the old man wouldn't recognize him. But he didn't want to be spotted by his two amazons who might feel refreshed enough by now to be ready for another tour of the town.

He needn't have worried. The ladies barely made it to the top of the stairs; they phoned for a cab and were presently whisked away. Dr. McAllen meanwhile also had made a telephone call, and settled down not far from Barney to wait. A small gray car, five or six years old but of polished and well-tended appearance, trundled presently up the pier, came into the turnaround at the boat station, and stopped. A thin old Negro, with hair as white as the doctor's, held the door open for McAllen. The car moved unhurriedly off with them.

The automobile's license number produced Dr. McAllen's California address for Barney a short while later. The physicist lived in Sweetwater Beach, fifteen minutes' drive from the pier, in an old Spanish-type house back in the hills. The chauffeur's name was John Emanuel Fredericks; he had been working for McAllen for an unknown length of time. No one else lived there.

Barney didn't bother with further details about the Sweetwater Beach establishment at the moment. The agencies he usually employed to dig up background information were reasonably trustworthy, but he wanted to attract no more attention than was necessary to his interest in Dr. McAllen.

That evening he took a plane to New York.

Physicist Frank Elby was a few years older than Barney, an acquaintance since their university days. Elby was ambitious, capable, slightly dishonest; on occasion he provided Barney with contraband information for which he was generously paid.

Over lunch Barney broached a business matter which would be financially rewarding to both of them, and should not burden Elby's conscience unduly. Elby reflected, and agreed. The talk became more general. Presently Barney remarked, "Ran into an old acquaintance of ours the other day. Remember Dr. McAllen?"

"Oliver B. McAllen? Naturally. Haven't heard about him in years. What's he doing?"

Barney said he had only seen the old man, hadn't spoken to him. But he was sure it was McAllen.

"Where was this?" Elby asked.

"Sweetwater Beach. Small town down the Coast."

Elby nodded. "It must have been McAllen. That's where he had his home."

"He was looking hale and hearty. They didn't actually institutionalize him at the time of his retirement, did they?"

"Oh, no. No reason for it. Except on the one subject of that cockeyed invention of his, he behaved perfectly normally. Besides he would have hired a lawyer and fought any such move. He had plenty of money. And nobody wanted publicity. McAllen was a pretty likable old boy."

"The university never considered taking him back?"

Elby laughed. "Well, hardly! After all, man—a matter transmitter!"

Barney felt an almost electric thrill of pleasure. Right on the nose, Brother Chard! Right on the nose.

He smiled. "Was that what it was supposed to be? I never was told all the details."

Elby said that for the few who were informed of the details it had been a seven-day circus. McAllen's reputation was such that more people, particularly on his staff, had been ready to believe him that were ready to admit it later. "When he'd left—you know, he never even bothered to take that 'transmitter' along—the thing was taken apart and checked over as carefully as if somebody thought it might still suddenly start working. But it was an absolute Goldberg, of course. The old man had simply gone off his rocker."

"Hadn't there been any indication of it before?"

"Not that I know of. Except that he'd been dropping hints about his gadget for several months before he showed it to anyone," Elby said indifferently. The talk turned to other things.

The rest was routine, not difficult to carry out. A small cottage on Mallorca, near the waterfront, was found to be in McAllen's name. McAllen's liquid assets were established to have dwindled to something less than those of John Emanuel Fredericks, who patronized the same local bank as his employer. There had been frequent withdrawals of large, irregular sums throughout the past years. The withdrawals were not explained by McAllen's frugal personal habits; even his fishing excursions showed an obvious concern for expense. The retention of the Mediterranean retreat, modest though it was, must have a reason beyond simple self-indulgence.

Barney arranged for the rental of a bungalow in the outskirts of Sweetwater beach, which lay uphill from the old house in which McAllen and Fredericks lived, and provided a good view of the residence and its street entry. He didn't go near the place himself. Operatives of a Los Angeles detective agency went on constant watch in the bungalow, with orders to photograph the two old men in the other house and any visitors at every appearance, and to record the exact times the pictures were taken. At the end of each day the photographs were delivered to an address from where they promptly reached Barney's hands.

A European agency was independently covering the Mallorca cottage in the same manner.

Nearly four weeks passed before Barney obtained the exact results he wanted. He called off the watch at both points, and next day came up the walk to McAllen's home and rang the doorbell. John Fredericks appeared, studied Barney's card and Barney with an air of mild disapproval, and informed him that Dr. McAllen did not receive visitors.

"So I've been told," Barney acknowledged pleasantly. "Please be so good as to give the doctor this."

Fredericks' white eyebrows lifted by the barest trifle as he looked at the sealed envelope Barney was holding out. After a moment's hesitation he took it, instructed Barney to wait, and closed the door firmly.

Listening to Fredericks' footsteps receding into the house, Barney lit a cigarette, and was pleased to find that his hands were as steady as if he had been on the most ordinary of calls. The envelope contained two sets of photographs, dated and indicating the time of day. The date was the same for both sets; the recorded time showed the pictures had been taken within fifteen minutes of one another. The central subject in each case was Dr. McAllen, sometimes accompanied by Fredericks. One set of photographs had been obtained on Mallorca, the other in Sweetwater Beach at McAllen's house.

Barring rocket assists, the two old men had been documented as the fastest moving human beings in all history.

Several minutes passed before Fredericks reappeared. With a face which was now completely without expression, he invited Barney to enter, and conducted him to McAllen's study. The scientist had the photographs spread out on a desk before him. He gestured at them.

"Just what—if anything—is this supposed to mean, sir?" he demanded in an unsteady voice.

Barney hesitated aware that Fredericks had remained in the hall just beyond the study. But Fredericks obviously was in McAllen's confidence. His eavesdropping could do no harm.

"It means this, doctor—" Barney began, amiably enough; and he proceeded to tell McAllen precisely what the photographs meant. McAllen broke in protestingly two or three times, then let Barney conclude his account of the steps he had taken to verify his farfetched hunch on the pier without further comment. After a few minutes Barney heard Fredericks' steps moving away, and then a door closing softly somewhere, and he shifted his position a trifle so that his right side was now toward the hall door. The little revolver was in the right-hand coat pocket. Even then Barney had no real concern that McAllen or Fredericks would attempt to resort to violence, but when people are acutely disturbed—and McAllen at least was—almost anything can happen.

When Barney finished, McAllen stared down at the photographs again, shook his head, and looked over at Barney.

"If you don't mind," he said, blinking behind his glasses, "I should like to think about this for a minute or two."

"Of course, doctor," Barney said politely. McAllen settled back in the chair, removed his glasses and half closed his eyes. Barney let his gaze rove. The furnishings of the house were what he had expected—well-tended, old, declining here and there to the downright shabby. The only reasonably new piece in the study was a radio-phonograph. The walls of the study and of the section of a living room he could see through a small archway were lined with crammed bookshelves. At the far end of the living room was a curious collection of clocks in various types and sizes, mainly antiques, but also some odd metallic pieces with modernistic faces. Vacancies in the rows indicated Fredericks might have begun to dispose discreetly of the more valuable items on his employer's behalf.

McAllen cleared his throat finally, opened his eyes, and settled the spectacles back on his nose.

"Mr. Chard," he inquired, "have you had scientific training?"

"No."

"Then," said McAllen, "the question remains of what your interest in the matter is. Perhaps you'd like to explain just why you put yourself to such considerable expense to intrude on my personal affairs—"

Barney hesitated perceptibly. "Doctor," he said, "there is something tantalizing about an enigma. I'm fortunate in having the financial means to gratify my curiosity when it's excited to the extent it was here."

McAllen nodded. "I can understand curiosity. Was that your only motive?"

Barney gave him his most disarming grin. "Frankly no. I've mentioned I'm a businessman—"

"Ah!" McAllen said, frowning.

"Don't misunderstand me. One of my first thoughts admittedly was that here were millions waiting to be picked up. But the investigation soon made a number of things clear to me."

"What were they?"

"Essentially, that you had so sound a reason for keeping your invention a secret that to do it you were willing to ruin yourself financially, and to efface yourself as a human being and as a scientist."

"I don't feel," McAllen observed mildly, "that I really have effaced myself, either as a human being or as a scientist."

"No, but as far as the public was concerned you did both."

McAllen smiled briefly. "That strategem was very effective—until now. Very well, Mr. Chard. You understand clearly that under no circumstances would I agree to the commercialization of ... well, of my matter transmitter?"

Barney nodded. "Of course."

"And you're still interested?"

"Very much so."

McAllen was silent for a few seconds, biting reflectively at his lower lip. "Very well," he said again. "You were speaking of my predilection for fishing. Perhaps you'd care to accompany me on a brief fishing trip?"

"Now?" Barney asked.

"Yes, now. I believe you understand what I mean ... I see you do. Then, if you'll excuse me for a few minutes—"

Barney couldn't have said exactly what he expected to be shown. His imaginings had run in the direction of a camouflaged vault beneath McAllen's house—some massively-walled place with machinery that powered the matter transmitter purring along the walls ... and perhaps something in the style of a plastic diving bell as the specific instrument of transportation.

The actual experience was quite different. McAllen returned shortly, having changed into the familiar outdoor clothing—apparently he had been literal about going on a fishing trip. Barney accompanied the old physicist into the living room, and watched him open a small but very sturdy wall safe. Immediately behind the safe door, an instrument panel had been built in the opening.

Peering over the spectacles, McAllen made careful adjustments on two sets of small dials, and closed and locked the safe again.

"Now, if you'll follow me, Mr. Chard—" He crossed the room to a door, opened it, and went out. Barney followed him into a small room with rustic furnishings and painted wooden walls. There was a single, heavily curtained window; the room was rather dim.

"Well," McAllen announced, "here we are."

It took a moment for that to sink in. Then, his scalp prickling eerily, Barney realized he was standing farther from the wall than he had thought. He looked around, and discovered there was no door behind him now, either open or closed.

He managed a shaky grin. "So that's how your matter transmitter works!"

"Well," McAllen said thoughtfully, "of course it isn't really a matter transmitter. I call it the McAllen Tube. Even an educated layman must realize that one can't simply disassemble a living body at one point, reassemble it at another, and expect life to resume. And there are other considerations—"

"Where are we?" Barney asked. "On Mallorca?"

"No. We haven't left the continent—just the state. Look out the window and see for yourself."

McAllen turned to a built-in closet, and Barney drew back the window hangings. Outside was a grassy slope, uncut and yellowed by the summer sun. The slope dropped sharply to a quiet lakefront framed by dark pines. There was no one in sight, but a small wooden dock ran out into the lake. At the far end of the dock an old rowboat lay tethered. And—quite obviously—it was no longer the middle of a bright afternoon; the air was beginning to dim, to shift towards evening.

Barney turned to find McAllen's mild, speculative eyes on him, and saw the old man had put a tackle box and fishing rod on the table.

"Your disclosures disturbed me more than you may have realized," McAllen remarked by way of explanation. His lips twitched in the shadow of a smile. "At such times I find nothing quite so soothing as to drop a line into water for a while. I've got some thinking to do, too. So let's get down to the dock. There ought to be a little bait left in the minnow pail."

When they returned to the cabin some time later, McAllen was in a pensive mood. He started a pot of coffee in the small kitchen, then quickly cleaned the tackle and put it away. Barney sat at the table, smoking and watching him, but made no attempt at conversation.

McAllen poured the coffee, produced sugar and powdered milk, and settled down opposite Barney. He said abruptly, "Have you had any suspicions about the reason for the secretive mumbo jumbo?"

"Yes," Barney said, "I've had suspicions. But it wasn't until *that* happened"—he waved his hand at the wall out of which they appeared to have stepped—"that I came to a definite conclusion."

"Eh?" McAllen's eyes narrowed suddenly. "What was the conclusion?"

"That you've invented something that's really a little too good."

"Too good?" said McAllen. "Hm-m-m. Go on."

"It doesn't take much power to operate the thing, does it?"

"Not," said McAllen dryly, "if you're talking about the kind of power one pays for."

"I am. Can the McAllen Tube be extended to any point on Earth?"

"I should think so."

"And you financed the building of this model yourself. Not very expensive. If the secret leaked out, I'd never know who was going to materialize in my home at any time, would I? Or with what intentions."

"That," McAllen nodded, "is about the size of it."

Barney crushed out his cigarette, lit a fresh one, blew out a thin streamer of smoke. "Under the circumstances," he remarked, "it's unfortunate you can't get the thing shut off again, isn't it?"

McAllen was silent for some seconds. "So you've guessed that, too," he said finally. "What mistake did I make?"

"None that I know of," Barney said. "But you're doing everything you can to keep the world from learning about the McAllen Tube. At the same time you've kept it in operation—which made it just a question of time before somebody else noticed something was going on, as I did. Your plans for the thing appear to have gone wrong."

McAllen was nodding glumly. "They have," he said. "They have, Mr. Chard. Not irreparably wrong, but still—" He paused. "The first time I activated the apparatus," he said, "I directed it only at two points. Both of them within structures which were and are my property. It was fortunate I did so."

"That was this cabin and the place on Mallorca?"

"Yes. The main operational sections of the Tube are concealed about my California home. But certain controls have to be installed at any exit point to make it possible to return. It wouldn't be easy to keep those hidden in any public place.

"It wasn't until I compared the actual performance of the Tube with my theoretical calculations that I discovered there was an unforeseen factor involved. To make it short, I could not—to use your phrasing—shut the Tube off again. But that would certainly involve some extremely disastrous phenomena at three different points of our globe."

"Explosions?" Barney asked.

"Weee-ll," McAllen said judiciously, "implosions might come a little closer to describing the effect. The exact term isn't contained in our vocabulary, and I'd prefer it *not* to show up there, at least in my lifetime. But you see my dilemma, don't you? If I asked for help, I revealed the existence of the Tube. Once its existence was known, the research that produced it could be duplicated. As you concluded, it isn't really too difficult a device to construct. And even with the present problem solved, the McAllen Tube is just a little too dangerous a thing to be at large in our world today."

"You feel the problem can be solved?"

"Oh, yes." McAllen took off his glasses and rubbed his eyes. "That part of it's only a matter of time. At first I thought I'd have everything worked out within three or four years. Unfortunately I badly underestimated the expense of some of the required experimentation. That's what's delayed everything."

"I see. I had been wondering," Barney admitted, "why a man with something like this on his mind would be putting in *quite* so much time fishing."

McAllen grinned. "Enforced idleness. It's been very irritating really, Mr. Chard. I've been obliged to proceed in the most inexpensive manner possible, and that meant—very slowly."

Barney said, "If it weren't for that question of funds, how long would it take to wind up the operation?"

"A year—perhaps two years." McAllen shrugged. "It's difficult to be too exact, but it certainly wouldn't be longer than two."

"And what would be the financial tab?"

McAllen hesitated. "A million is the bottom figure, I'm afraid. It should run closer to a million and a half."

"Doctor," Barney said, "let me make you a proposition."

McAllen looked at him. "Are you thinking of financing the experiments, Mr. Chard?"

"In return," Barney said, "for a consideration."

"What's that?" McAllen's expression grew wary.

"When you retired," Barney told him, "I dropped a nice piece of money as a consequence. It was the first beating I'd taken, and it hurt. I'd like to pick that money up again. All right. We're agreed it can't be done on the McAllen Tube. The Tube wouldn't help make the world a safer place for Barney Chard. But the Tube isn't any more remarkable than the mind that created it. Now I know a company which could be top of the heap in electronics precision work—one-shot specialties is what they go in for—if it had your mind as technical advisor. I can buy a controlling interest in that company tomorrow, doctor. And you can have the million and a half paid off in not much more time than you expect to take to get your monster back under control and shut down. Three years of your technical assistance, and we're clear."

McAllen's face reddened slowly. "I've considered hiring out, of course," he said. "Many times. I need the money very badly. But aren't you overlooking something?"

"What?"

"I went to considerable pains," said McAllen, "to establish myself as a lunatic. It was distasteful, but it seemed necessary to discourage anyone from making too close an investigation of some of my more recent lines of research. If it became known now that I was again in charge of a responsible project—"

Barney shook his head. "No problem, doctor. We'd be drawing on outside talent for help in specific matters—very easy to cover up any leads to you personally. I've handled that general sort of thing before."

McAllen frowned thoughtfully. "I see. But I'd have—There wouldn't be so much work that—"

"No," Barney said. "I guarantee that you'll have all the time you want for your own problem." He smiled. "Considering what you told me, I'd like to hear that one's been solved myself!"

McAllen grinned briefly. "I can imagine. Very well. Ah ... when can you let me have the money, Mr. Chard?"

The sun was setting beyond the little lake as Barney drew the shades over the cabin window again. Dr. McAllen was half inside the built-in closet at the moment, fitting a pair of toggle switches to the concealed return device in there.

"Here we go," he said suddenly.

Three feet from the wall of the room the shadowy suggestion of another wall, and of an open door, became visible.

Barney said dubiously, "We came out of *that?*"

McAllen looked at him, sad, "The appearance is different on the exit side. But the Tube's open now—Here, I'll show you."

He went up to the apparition of a door, abruptly seemed to melt into it. Barney held his breath, and followed. Again there was no sensory reaction to passing through the Tube. As his foot came down on something solid in the shadowiness into which he stepped, the living room in Sweetwater Beach sprang into sudden existence about him.

"Seems a little odd from that end, the first time through, doesn't it?" McAllen remarked.

Barney let out his breath.

"If I'd been the one who invented the Tube," he said honestly, "I'd never have had the nerve to try it."

McAllen grinned. "Tell you the truth, I did need a drink or two the first time. But it's dead-safe if you know just what you're doing."

Which was not, Barney felt, too reassuring. He looked back. The door through which they had come was the one by which they had left. But beyond it now lay a section of the entrance hall of the Sweetwater Beach house.

"Don't let that fool you," said McAllen, following his gaze. "If you tried to go out into the hall at the moment, you'd find yourself right back in the cabin. Light rays passing through the Tube can be shunted off and on." He went over to the door, closed and locked it, dropping the key in his pocket. "I keep it locked. I don't often have visitors, but if I had one while the door was open it could be embarrassing."

"What about the other end?" Barney asked. "The door appeared in the cabin when you turned those switches. What happens now? Suppose someone breaks into the cabin and starts prowling around—is the door still there?"

McAllen shook his head. "Not unless that someone happened to break in within the next half-minute." He considered. "Let's put it this way. The Tube's permanently centered on its two exit points, but the effect ordinarily is dissipated over half a mile of the neighborhood at the other end. For practical purposes there is no useful effect. When I'm going to go through, I bring the exit end down to a focus point ... does that make sense? Very well. It remains focused for around sixty or ninety seconds, depending on how I set it; then it expands again." He nodded at the locked door. "In the cabin, that's disappeared by now. Walk through the space where it's been, and you'll notice nothing unusual. Clear?"

Barney hesitated. "And if that door were still open here, and somebody attempted to step through after the exit end had expanded—"

"Well," McAllen said, moving over to a wall buzzer and pressing it, "that's what I meant when I said it could be embarrassing. He'd get expanded too—disastrously. Could you use a drink, Mr. Chard? I know I want one."

The drinks, served by Fredericks, were based on a rather rough grade of bourbon, but Barney welcomed them. There was an almost sick fascination in what was a certainty now: he was going to get the Tube. That tremendous device was his for the taking. He was well inside McAllen's guard; only carelessness could arouse the old man's suspicions again, and Barney was not going to be careless. No need to hurry anything. He would play the reserved role he had selected for himself, leave developments up to the fact that McAllen had carried the burden of his secret for twelve years, with no more satisfactory confidant than Fredericks to trust with it. Having told Barney so much, McAllen wanted to tell more. He would have needed very little encouragement to go on talking about it now.

Barney offered no encouragement. Instead, he gave McAllen a cautiously worded reminder that it was not inconceivable they had an audience here, at which McAllen reluctantly subsided. There was, however, one fairly important question Barney still wanted answered today. The nature of the answer would tell him the manner in which McAllen should now be handled.

He waited until he was on his feet and ready to leave before presenting it. McAllen's plump cheeks were flushed from the two highballs he had put away; in somewhat awkward phrases he had been expressing his gratitude for Barney's generous help, and his relief that because of it the work on the Tube now could be brought to an end.

"Just one thing about that still bothers me a little, doctor," Barney said candidly.

McAllen looked concerned. "What's that, Mr. Chard?"

"Well ... you're in good health, I'd say." Barney smiled. "But suppose something did happen to you before you succeeded in shutting the McAllen Tube down." He inclined his head toward the locked door.

"That thing would still be around waiting for somebody to open it and step through...."

McAllen's expression of concern vanished. He dug a forefinger cheerfully into Barney's ribs. "Young man, you needn't worry. I've been aware of the possibility, of course, and believe me I'm keeping *very* careful notes and instructions. Safe deposit boxes ... we'll talk about that tomorrow, eh? Somewhere else? Had a man in mind, as a matter of fact, but we can make better arrangements now. You see, it's really so ridiculously *easy* at this stage."

Barney cleared his throat. "Some other physicist—?"

"*Any* capable physicist," McAllen said decidedly. "Just a matter, you see of how reliable he is." He winked at Barney. "Talk about that tomorrow too—or one of these days."

Barney stood looking down, with a kind of detached surprise, at a man who had just pronounced sentence of death casually on himself, and on an old friend. For the first time in Barney's career, the question of deliberate murder not only entered an operation, but had become in an instant an unavoidable part of it. Frank Elby, ambitious and money-hungry, could take over where McAllen left off. Elby was highly capable, and Elby could be controlled. McAllen could not. He could only be tricked; and, if necessary, killed.

It was necessary, of course. If McAllen lived until he knew how to shut the Tube down safely, he simply would shut it down, destroy the device and his notes on it. A man who had gone to such extreme lengths to safeguard the secret was not going to be talked out of his conviction that the McAllen Tube was a menace to the world. Fredericks, the morose eavesdropper, had to be silenced with his employer to assure Barney of his undisputed possession of the Tube.

Could he still let the thing go, let McAllen live? He couldn't, Barney decided. He'd dealt himself a hand in a new game, and a big one—a fantastic, staggering game when one considered the possibilities in the Tube. It meant new interest, it meant life for him. It wasn't in his nature to pull out. The part about McAllen was cold necessity. A very ugly necessity, but McAllen— pleasantly burbling something as they walked down the short hall to the front door—already seemed a little unreal, a roly-poly, muttering, fading small ghost.

In the doorway Barney exchanged a few words—he couldn't have repeated them an instant later—with the ghost, became briefly aware of a remarkably firm hand clasp, and started down the cement walk to the street. Evening had come to California at last; a few houses across the street made dim silhouettes against the hills, some of the windows lit. He felt, Barney realized, curiously tired and depressed. A few steps behind him, he heard McAllen quietly closing the door to his home.

The walk, the garden, the street, the houses and hills beyond, vanished in a soundlessly violent explosion of white light around Barney Chard.

His eyes might have been open for several seconds before he became entirely aware of the fact. He was on his back looking up at the low raftered ceiling of a room. The light was artificial, subdued; it gave the impression of nighttime outdoors.

Memory suddenly blazed up. "Tricked!" came the first thought. Outsmarted. Outfoxed. And by—Then that went lost in a brief, intense burst of relief at the realization he was still alive, apparently unhurt. Barney turned sharply over on his side—bed underneath, he discovered—and stared around.

The room was low, wide. Something undefinably odd—He catalogued it quickly. Redwood walls, Navaho rugs on the floor, bookcases, unlit fireplace, chairs, table, desk with a typewriter and reading lamp. Across the room a tall dark grandfather clock with a bright metal disk instead of a clock-face stood against the wall. From it came a soft, low thudding as deliberate as the heartbeat of some big animal. It was the twin of one of the clocks he had seen in McAllen's living room.

The room was McAllen's, of course. Almost luxurious by comparison with his home, but wholly typical of the man. And now Barney became aware of its unusual feature; there were no windows. There was one door, so far to his right he had to twist his head around to see it. It stood half open; beyond it a few feet of a narrow passage lay within his range of vision, lighted in the same soft manner as the room. No sound came from there.

Had he been left alone? And what had happened? He wasn't in McAllen's home or in that fishing shack at the lake. The Tube might have picked him up—somehow—in front of McAllen's house, transported him to the Mallorca place. Or he might be in a locked hideaway McAllen had built beneath the Sweetwater Beach house.

Two things were unpleasantly obvious. His investigations hadn't revealed all of McAllen's secrets. And the old man hadn't really been fooled by Barney Chard's smooth approach. Not, at any rate, to the extent of deciding to trust him.

Hot chagrin at the manner in which McAllen had handed the role of dupe back to him flooded Barney for a moment. He swung his legs over the side of the bed and stood up. His coat had been hung neatly over the back of a chair a few feet away; his shoes stood next to the bed. Otherwise he was fully clothed. Nothing in the pockets of the coat appeared to have been touched; billfold, cigarette case, lighter, even the gun, were in place; the gun, almost startlingly, was still loaded. Barney thrust the revolver thoughtfully into his trousers pocket. His wrist watch seemed to be the only item missing.

He glanced about the room again, then at the half-open door and the stretch of narrow hallway beyond. McAllen must have noticed the gun. The fact that he hadn't bothered to take it away, of at least to unload it, might have been reassuring under different circumstances. Here, it could have a very disagreeable meaning. Barney went quietly to the door, stood listening a few seconds, became convinced there was no one within hearing range, and moved on down the hall.

In less than two minutes he returned to the room, with the first slow welling of panic inside him. He had found a bathroom, a small kitchen and pantry, a storage room twice as wide and long as the rest of the place combined, crammed with packaged and crated articles, and with an attached freezer. If it was mainly stored food, as Barney thought, and if there was adequate ventilation and independent power, as seemed to be the case, then McAllen had constructed a superbly self-sufficient hideout. A man might live comfortably enough for years without emerging from it.

There was only one thing wrong with the setup from Barney's point of view. The thing he'd been afraid of. Nowhere was there an indication of a window or of an exit door.

The McAllen Tube, of course, might make such ordinary conveniences unnecessary. And if the Tube was the only way in or out, then McAllen incidentally had provided himself with an escape-proof jail for anyone he preferred to keep confined. The place might very well have been built several hundred feet underground. A rather expensive proposition but, aside from that, quite feasible.

Barney felt his breath begin to quicken, and told himself to relax. Wherever he was, he shouldn't be here long. McAllen presently would be getting in contact with him. And then—

His glance touched the desk across the room, and now he noticed his missing wrist watch on it. He went over, picked it up, and discovered that the long white envelope on which the watch had been placed was addressed to him.

For a moment he stared at the envelope. Then, his fingers shaking a little, he tore open the envelope and pulled out the typewritten sheets within.

The letterhead, he saw without surprise, was OLIVER B. MCALLEN.

The letter read:

Dear Mr. Chard:

An unfortunate series of circumstances, combined with certain character traits in yourself, make it necessary to inconvenience you in a rather serious manner.

To explain: The information I gave you regarding the McAllen Tube and my own position was not entirely correct. It is not the intractable instrument I presented it as being—it can be "shut off" again quite readily and without any attendant difficulties. Further, the decision to conceal its existence was not reached by myself alone. For years we—that is, Mr. Fredericks, who holds a degree in engineering and was largely responsible for the actual construction of the Tube—and I, have been members of an association of which I cannot tell you too much. But I may say that it acts, among other things, as the present custodian of some of the more dangerous products of human science, and will continue to do so until a more stable period permits their safe release.

To keep developments such as the McAllen Tube out of irresponsible hands is no easy task these days, but a variety of effective devices are employed to that end. In this instance, you happened upon a "rigged" situation, which had been designed to draw action from another man, an intelligent and unscrupulous individual who lately had indicated a disturbing interest in events connected with the semipublic fiasco of my "matter transmitter" some years ago. The chances of another person becoming aware of the temporal incongruities which were being brought to this man's attention were regarded as so remote that they need be given no practical consideration. Nevertheless, the unexpected happened: you became interested. The promptness with which you acted on your chance observations shows a bold and imaginative manner of thinking on which you may be genuinely congratulated.

However, a perhaps less commendable motivation was also indicated. While I appeared to stall on coming to decisions you may have regarded as inevitable, your background was being investigated by the association. The investigation confirmed that you fall within a personality category of which we have the greatest reason to be wary.

Considering the extent of what you had surmised and learned, falsified though the picture was, this presented a serious problem. It was made more acute by the fact that the association is embarking on a "five-year-plan" of some importance. Publicity during this period would be more than ordinarily undesirable. It will therefore be necessary to see to it that you have no opportunity to tell what you know before the plan is concluded. I am sure you can see it would be most unwise to accept your simple word on the matter. Your freedom of movement and of communication must remain drastically restricted until this five-year period is over.

Within the next two weeks, as shown by the clock in your quarters, it will have become impossible for me or for any member of the association to contact you again before the day of your release. I tell you this so that you will not nourish vain hopes of changing the situation in your favor, but will adjust as rapidly as you can to the fact that you must spend the next five years by yourself. What ameliorations of this basic condition appeared possible have been provided.

It is likely that you will already have tried to find a way out of the cabin in which you were left. The manner of doing this will become apparent to you exactly twenty-four hours after I conclude and seal this letter. It seemed best to advise you of some details of your confinement before letting you discover that you have been given as much limited freedom as circumstances allowed.

Sincerely yours,
OLIVER B. MCALLEN

Barney dropped the letter on the desk, stared down at it, his mouth open. His face had flushed red. "Why, he's crazy!" he said aloud at last. "He's crazier than—" He straightened, looked uneasily about the room again.

Whether a maniac McAllen made a more desirable jailer than a secret association engaged in keeping dangerous scientific developments under cover could be considered an open question. The most hopeful thought was that Dr. McAllen was indulging an unsuspected and nasty sense of humor.

Unfortunately, there wasn't the slightest reason to believe it. McAllen was wise to him. The situation was no gag—and neither was it necessarily what McAllen wanted him to think. Unless his watch had been reset, he had been knocked out by whatever hit him for roughly five hours—or seventeen, he amended. But he would have been hungry if it had been the longer period; and he wasn't.

Five hours then. Five hours wouldn't have given them time to prepare the "cabin" as it was prepared: for someone's indefinite stay. At a guess, McAllen had constructed it as a secure personal retreat in the event of something like a nuclear holocaust. But, in that case, why vacate it now for Barney Chard?

Too many questions, he thought. Better just keep looking around.

The blank metal face on the grandfather clock swung back to reveal a group of four dials, each graduated in a different manner, only one of them immediately familiar. Barney studied the other three for some seconds, then their meaning suddenly came clear. The big clock had just finished softly talking away the fourth hour of the first day of the first month of Year One. There were five figures on the Year Dial.

He stared at it. A five-year period of—something seemed to be the key to the entire setup.

Barney shook his head. Key it might be, but not one he could read without additional data. He snapped the cover disk shut on the unpleasantly suggestive dials, and began to go mentally over McAllen's letter.

The business that in twenty-four hours—twenty now—the manner of leaving the cabin would become "apparent" to him—that seemed to dispose of the possibility of being buried underground here. McAllen would hardly have provided him with a personal model of the Tube; he must be speaking of an ordinary door opening on the immediate environment, equipped with a time lock.

In that case, where was the door?

Barney made a second, far more careful search. Three hours later, he concluded it. He'd still found no trace of an exit. But the paneling in any of the rooms might slide aside to reveal one at the indicated time, or a section of the floor might swing back above a trap door. There was no point in attempting to press the search any further. After all, he only had to wait.

On the side, he'd made other discoveries. After opening a number of crates in the storage room, and checking contents of the freezer, he could assume that there was in fact more than enough food here to sustain one man for five years. Assuming the water supply held out—there was no way of checking on it; the source of the water like that of the power and the ventilation lay outside the area which was accessible to him—but if the water could be depended on, he wouldn't go hungry or thirsty. Even tobacco and liquor were present in comparably liberal quantities. The liquor he'd seen was all good; almost at random he had selected a bottle of cognac and brought it and a glass to the main room with him. The thought of food wasn't attractive at the moment. But he could use a drink.

He half filled the glass, emptied it with a few swallows, refilled it and took it over to one of the armchairs. He began to feel more relaxed almost at once. But the truth was, he acknowledged, settling back in the chair, that the situation was threatening to unnerve him completely. Everything he'd seen implied McAllen's letter came close to stating the facts; what wasn't said became more alarming by a suggestion of deliberate vagueness. Until that melodramatically camouflaged door was disclosed—seventeen hours from now—he'd be better off if he didn't try to ponder the thing out.

And the best way to do that might be to take a solid load on rapidly, and then sleep away as much of the intervening time as possible.

He wasn't ordinarily a hard drinker, but he'd started on the second bottle before the cabin began to blur on him. Afterwards, he didn't remember making it over to the bed.

Barney woke up ravenous and without a trace of hangover. Making a mental adjustment to his surroundings took no more time than opening his eyes; he'd been dreaming Dr. McAllen had dropped him into a snake pit and was sadistically dangling a rope twelve feet above his head, inviting him to climb out. To find himself still in the softly lit cabin was—for a few seconds, at any rate—a relief.

The relief faded as he sat up and looked at his watch. Still over an hour to go before McAllen's idiotic door became "apparent." Barney swore and headed for the bathroom to freshen up.

There was an electric shaver there, the end of its cord vanishing into the wall. Barney used it as meticulously as if he were embarking on a day of normal activities, prepared a breakfast in the kitchen and took it to the main room. He ate unhurriedly, absorbed in his thoughts, now and then glancing about the room. After a few minutes he uneasily pushed back the plate and stood up. If McAllen's twenty-four hours began with the moment the big clock in the room had been started, the door should be in evidence by now.

Another tour of the place revealed nothing and left him nervous enough to start biting his nails. He moved about the room, looking over things he'd already investigated. A music cabinet—he'd thought it was a radio at first, but it was only an elaborate hi-fi record player; two enclosed racks of records went with it—mainly classical stuff apparently. And a narrow built-in closet with three polished fishing rods and related gear, which would have allowed for speculation on the nature of the cabin's surroundings, except that McAllen might feel compelled to have a sampling of his toys around him wherever he was. Barney closed the closet door morosely, stood regarding the two crowded bookcases next to it. Plenty of books—reflecting the

McAllen taste again. Technical tomes. Great Literature. Dickens, Melville, the Life of Gandhi.

Barney grunted, and was turning away when another title caught his eye. He glanced back at it, hauled out the book:

"Fresh Water Game Fish; Tested Methods of Their Pursuit." The author: O. B. McAllen.

Barney was opening the book when the cabin's door also opened.

Bright light—daylight—filled the room with so sudden a gush that Barney's breath caught in his throat. The book seemed to leap out of his hands. With the same glance he saw then the low, wide picture window which abruptly had appeared in the opposite wall, occupying almost half its space—and, in the other wall on the far left, a big door which was still swinging slowly open into the room. Daylight poured in through window and door. And beyond them—

For seconds he stared at the scene outside, barely aware of what he was looking at, while his mind raced on. He had searched every inch of the walls. And those thick wooden panels hadn't simply slid aside; the surfaces of doorframe and window were flush with the adjoining wall sections. So the McAllen Tube was involved in these changes in the room—and he might have guessed, Barney thought, that McAllen would have found more than one manner of putting the space-twisting properties of his device to use. And then finally he realized what he was seeing through the window and beyond the door. He walked slowly up to the window, still breathing unevenly.

The scene was unfamiliar but not at all extraordinary. The cabin appeared to be part way up one side of a heavily forested, rather narrow valley. It couldn't be more than half a mile to the valley's far slope which rose very steeply, almost like a great cresting green wave, filling the entire window. Coming closer Barney saw the skyline above it, hazy, summery, brilliantly luminous. This cabin of McAllen's might be in one of the wilder sections of the Canadian Rockies.

Or—and this was a considerably less happy thought—it probably could have been set up just as well in some area like the Himalayas.

But a more immediate question was whether the cabin actually *was* in the valley or only appearing to be there. The use of the Tube made it possible that this room and its seeming surroundings were very far apart in fact. And just what would happen to him then if he decided to step outside?

There were scattered sounds beyond the open door: bird chirpings and whistles, and the continuous burring calls of what Barney decided would be a wild pigeon. Then a swirl of wind stirred the nearer branches. He could feel the wash of the breeze in the room.

It looked and sounded—and felt—all right.

Barney scowled undecidedly, clearing his throat, then discovered that a third item had appeared in the room along with the door and the window. In the wall just this side of the door at shoulder-height was a small ivory plate with two black switches on it. Presumably the controls for door and window....

Barney went over, gingerly touched the one on the right, watching the window; then flicked up the switch. Instantly, the window had vanished, the wood paneling again covered the wall. Barney turned the switch down. The window was back.

The door refused to disappear until he pushed it shut. Then it obeyed its switch with the same promptness.

He went back across the room, returned with one of McAllen's fishing poles, and edged its tip tentatively out through the door. He wouldn't have been surprised if the tip had disintegrated in that instant. But nothing at all occurred. He dug about with the pole in the loose earth beyond the doorsill, then drew it back. The breeze was flowing freely past him; a few grains of soil blew over the sill and into the room. The door seemed to be concealing no grisly tricks and looked to be safe enough.

Barney stepped out on the sill, moved on a few hesitant steps, stood looking about. He had a better view of the valley here—and the better view told him immediately that he was not in the Canadian Rockies. At least, Canada, to his knowledge, had no desert. And, on the left, this valley came to an end perhaps a little more than a mile away from the cabin, its wooded slopes flowing steeply down to a landscape which was dull rust-red—flat sand stretches alternating with worn rock escarpments, until the desert's rim rose toward and touched the hazy white sky. Not so very different from—

Barney's eyes widened suddenly. Could he be in the Sierras—perhaps not more than three or four hours' drive from Los Angeles?

Three or four hours' drive if he'd had a car, or course. But even so—

He stared around, puzzled. There were no signs of a human being, of human habitation. But somebody else must be here. Somebody to keep guard on him. Otherwise there was nothing to stop him from walking away from this place—though it might very well be a long, uncomfortable hike to any civilized spot.

Even if this did turn out to be the Himalayas, or some equally remote area, there must be hill tribes about if one went far enough—there should even be an occasional airplane passing overhead.

Barney stood just outside the door, frowning, pondering the situation again, searching for the catch in it. McAllen and his friends, whatever else they might be, weren't stupid. There was something involved here that he hadn't become aware of yet.

Almost without thought then, he turned up his head, squinting at the bright hazy sky above him—

And saw IT.

His breath sucked in and burst from his lungs in a half-strangled, terrified squawk as he staggered backward into the cabin, slammed the door shut, then spun around and began slapping frantically at the switches on the wall-plate until door and window were gone, and only the cabin's soft illumination was around him again. Then he crouched on the floor, his back against the wall, shaking with a terror he could hardly have imagined before.

He knew what the catch was now. He had understood it completely in the instant of glancing up and seeing that tiny brilliant blue-white point of light glare down at him through the incandescent cloud layers above. Like a blazing, incredibly horrible insect eye....

This world's sun.

THE END OF YEAR ONE

Barney Chard came up out of an uneasy sleep to the sudden sharp awareness that something was wrong. For some seconds he lay staring about the unlit cabin, mouth dry, heart hammering with apprehension. Then he discovered it was only that he had left the exit door open and the window switched on.... Only? This was the first time since they had left him here that he had gone to sleep without sealing the cabin first—even when blind drunk, really embalmed.

He thought of climbing out of bed and taking care of it now, but decided to let the thing ride. After all he knew there was nothing in the valley—nothing, in fact, on this world—of which he had a realistic reason to be afraid. And he felt dead tired. Weak and sick. Feeling like that no longer alarmed him as it had done at first; it was a simple physical fact. The sheet under him was wet with sweat, though it was no more than comfortably warm in the room. The cabin never became more than comfortably warm. Barney lay back again, trying to figure out how it had happened he had forgotten about the window and the door.

It had been night for quite a while when he went to sleep, but regardless of how long he'd slept, it was going to go on being night a good deal longer. The last time he had bothered to check—which, Barney decided on reflection, might be several months ago now—the sunless period had continued for better than fifty-six hours. Not long before dropping on the bed, he was standing in front of the big clock while the minute hand on the hour dial slid up to the point which marked the end of the first year in Earth time he had spent in the cabin. Watching it happen, he was suddenly overwhelmed again by the enormity of his solitude, and it looked as if it were going to turn into another of those periods when he sat with the gun in his hand, sobbing and swearing in a violent muddle of self-pity and helpless fury. He decided to knock off the lamenting and get good and drunk instead. And he would make it a drunk to top all drunks on this happy anniversary night.

But he hadn't done that either. He had everything set up, downright festively—glasses, crushed ice, a formidable little squad of fresh bottles. But when he looked at the array, he suddenly felt sick in advance. Then there was a wave of leaden heaviness, of complete fatigue. He hadn't had time to think of sealing the cabin. He had simply fallen into the bed then and there, and for all practical purposes passed out on the spot.

Barney Chard lay wondering about that. It had been, one might say, a rough year. Through the long days in particular, he had been doing his level best to obliterate his surroundings behind sustained fogs of alcoholism. The thought of the hellishly brilliant far-off star around which this world circled, the awareness that only the roof and walls of the cabin were between himself and that blazing alien watcher, seemed entirely unbearable. The nights, after a while, were easier to take. They had their strangeness too, but the difference wasn't so great. He grew accustomed to the big green moon, and developed almost an affection for a smaller one, which was butter-yellow and on an orbit that made it a comparatively infrequent visitor in the sky over the valley. By night he began to leave the view window in operation and finally even the door open for hours at a time. But he had never done it before when he wanted to go to sleep.

Alcoholism, Barney decided, stirring uneasily on the sweat-soiled, wrinkled sheet, hadn't been much of a success. His body, or perhaps some resistant factor in his mind, let him go so far and no farther. When he exceeded the limit, he became suddenly and violently ill. And remembering the drunk periods wasn't pleasant. Barney Chard, that steel-tough lad, breaking up, going to pieces, did not make a pretty picture. It was when he couldn't keep that picture from his mind that he most frequently had sat there with the gun, turning it slowly around in his hand. It had been a rather close thing at times.

Perhaps he simply hated McAllen and the association too much to use the gun. Drunk or sober, he brooded endlessly over methods of destroying them. He had to be alive when they came back. Some while ago there had been a space of several days when he was hallucinating the event, when McAllen and the association seemed to be present, and he was arguing with them, threatening them, even pleading with them. He came out of that period deeply frightened by what he was doing. Since then he hadn't been drinking as heavily.

But this was the first time he'd gone to sleep without drinking at all.

He sat up on the edge of the bed, found himself shaking a little again after that minor effort, but climbed to his feet anyway, and walked unsteadily over to the door. He stood there looking out. The cloud layers always faded away during the night, gathered again at dawn. By now the sky was almost clear. A green glow over the desert to the left meant the larger moon was just below the horizon. The little yellow moon rode high in the sky above it. If they came up together, this would be the very bright part of the night during which the birds and other animal life in the valley went about their pursuits as if it were daytime. He could hear bird-chirpings now against the restless mutter of the little stream which came down the center of the valley, starting at the lake at the right end and running out into stagnant and drying pools a short distance after it entered the desert.

He discovered suddenly he had brought the gun along from the bed with him and was holding it without having been in the least aware of the fact. Grinning twistedly at the old and pointless precaution, he shoved the gun into his trousers pocket, brought out matches, a crumpled pack of cigarettes, and began to smoke. Very considerate of them to see to it he wouldn't run out of minor conveniences ... like leaving him liquor enough to drink himself to death on any time he felt like it during these five years.

Like leaving him the gun—

From the association's standpoint those things were up to him, of course, Barney thought bitterly. In either unfortunate event, he wouldn't be on *their* consciences.

He felt a momentary spasm of the old hate, but a feeble one, hardly more than a brief wash of the early torrents of rage. Something had burned out of him these months; an increasing dullness was moving into its place—

And just what, he thought, startled, was he doing outside the cabin door now? He hadn't consciously decided to go that far; it must have been months, actually, since he had walked beyond the doorway at all. During the first few weeks he had made half a dozen attempts to explore his surroundings by night, and learned quickly that he was confined to as much of the valley as he could see from the cabin. Beyond the ridges lay naked desert and naked mountain ranges, silent and terrifying in the moonlight.

Barney glanced up and down the valley, undecided but not knowing quite what he was undecided about. He didn't feel like going back into the cabin, and to just stand here was boring.

"Well," he said aloud, sardonically, "it's a nice night for a walk, Brother Chard."

Well, why not? It was bright enough to see by now if he kept away from the thickest growths of trees, and getting steadily brighter as the big moon moved up behind the distant desert rim. He'd walk till he got tired, then rest. By the time he got back to the cabin he'd be ready to lie down and sleep off the curious mood that had taken hold of him.

Barney started off up the valley, stepping carefully and uncertainly along the sloping, uneven ground.

During the early weeks he had found a thick loose-leaf binder in the back of one of the desk drawers. He thought it might have been left there intentionally. Its heading was NOTES ON THE TERRESTRIAL ECOLOGICAL BASE OF THE EIGHTEENTH SYSTEM, VOLUME

III. After leafing through them once, it had been a while before Barney could bring himself to study the notes in more detail. He didn't, at that time, want to know too much about the situation he was in. He was still numbed by it.

But eventually he went over the binder carefully. The various reports were unsigned, but appeared to have been compiled by at least four or five persons—McAllen among them; his writing style was not difficult to recognize. Leaving out much that was incomprehensible or nearly so, Barney could still construe a fairly specific picture of the association project of which he was now an unscheduled and unwilling part. Selected plants and animals had been moved from Earth through the McAllen Tube to a world consisting of sand, rock and water, without detected traces of indigenous life in any form. At present the Ecological Base was only in its ninth year, which meant that the larger trees in the valley had been nearly full-grown when brought here with the soil that was to nourish them. From any viewpoint, the planting of an oasis of life on the barren world had been a gigantic undertaking, but there were numerous indications that the McAllen Tube was only one of the array of improbable devices the association had at its disposal for such tasks. A few cryptic paragraphs expressed the writer's satisfaction with the undetailed methods by which the Base's localized climatic conditions were maintained.

So far even the equipment which kept the cabin in uninterrupted operation had eluded Barney's search. It and the other required machinery might be buried somewhere in the valley. Or it might, he thought, have been set up just as easily some distance away, in the desert or among the remotely towering mountain ranges. One thing he had learned from the binder was that McAllen had told the truth in saying no one could contact him from Earth before the full period of his exile was over. The reason had seemed appalling enough in itself. This world had moved to a point in its orbit where the radiance of its distant sun was thickening between it and Earth, growing too intense to be penetrated by the forces of the McAllen Tube. Another four years would pass before the planet and the valley emerged gradually from behind that barrier again.

He walked, rested, walked again. Now and then he was troubled by a burst of violent sweating, followed by shivering fits until his clothes began to dry again. The big moon edged presently over the ridge above him, and in the first flood of its light the opposite slope of the valley took on the appearance of a fanciful sub-oceanic reef. The activity of the animal life about Barney increased promptly. It was no darker now than an evening hour on Earth, and his fellow occupants of the Ecological Base seemed well-adjusted to the strange shifts of day and night to which they had been consigned.

He pushed through a final thicket of shrubbery, and found himself at the edge of the lake. Beyond the almost circular body of water, a towering wall of cliffs sealed the upper end of the valley. He had come almost a mile, and while a mile—a city mile, at least—wouldn't have meant much to Barney Chard at one time, he felt quite exhausted now. He sat down at the edge of the water, and, after a minute or two, bent forward and drank from it. It had the same cold, clear flavor as the water in the cabin.

The surface of the water was unquiet. Soft-flying large insects of some kind were swarming about, stippling the nearby stretch of the lake with their touch, and there were frequent swift swirls as fish rose from beneath to take down the flyers. Presently one of them broke clear into the air—a big fish, thick-bodied and shining, looking as long as Barney's arm in the moonlight—and dropped back with a splash. Barney grinned twistedly. The NOTES indicated Dr. McAllen had taken some part in stocking the valley, and one could trust McAllen to see to it that the presence of his beloved game fish wasn't overlooked even in so outlandish a project.

He shifted position, became aware of the revolver in his pocket and brought it out. A wave of dull anger surged slowly through him again. What they did with trees and animals was their own business. But what they had done to a human being....

He scrambled suddenly to his feet, drew his arm back, and sent the gun flying far out over the lake. It spun through the moonlight, dipped, struck the surface with less of a splash than the fish had made, and was gone.

Now why, Barney asked himself in amazement, did I do that? He considered it a moment, and then, for the first time in over a year, felt a brief touch of something not far from elation.

He wasn't going to die here. No matter how politely the various invitations to do himself in had been extended by McAllen or the association, he was going to embarrass them by being alive and healthy when they came back to the valley four years from now. They wouldn't kill him then; they'd already shown they didn't have the guts to commit murder directly. They would have to take him back to Earth.

And once he was there, it was going to be too bad for them. It didn't matter how closely they watched him; in the end he would find or make the opportunity to expose them, pull down the whole lousy, conceited crew, see them buried under the shambles an outraged world would make of the secret association....

THE END OF YEAR TWO

The end of Year Two on the Ecological Base in the Eighteenth System arrived and went by without Barney's being immediately aware of the fact. Some two hours later, he glanced at his wrist watch, pushed back the chair, got up from the desk and went over to the big grandfather clock to confirm his surmise.

"Well, well, Brother Chard," he said aloud. "Another anniversary ... and three of them to go. We're almost at the halfway mark—"

He snapped the cover plate back over the multiple clock faces, and turned away. Three more years on the Ecological Base was a gruesome stretch of time when you thought of it as a whole....

Which was precisely why he rarely let himself think of it as a whole nowadays.

This last year, at any rate, Barney conceded to himself, had to be regarded as an improvement on the first. Well, he added irritably, and what wouldn't be? It hadn't been delightful, he'd frequently felt almost stupefied with boredom. But physically, at least, he was fit—considerably fitter, as a matter of fact, than he'd ever been in his life.

Not very surprising. When he got too restless to be able to settle down to anything else, he was walking about the valley, moving along at his best clip regardless of obstacles until he was ready to drop to the ground wherever he was. Exertion ate up restlessness eventually—for a while. Selecting another tree to chop into firewood took the edge off the spasms of rage that tended to come up if he started thinking too long about that association of jerks somewhere beyond the sun. Brother Chard was putting on muscle all over. And after convincing himself at last—after all, the animals weren't getting hurt—that the glaring diamond of fire in the daytime sky couldn't really be harmful, he had also rapidly put on a Palm Beach tan. When his carefully rationed sleep periods eventually came around, he was more than ready for them, and slept like a log.

Otherwise: projects. Projects to beat boredom, and never mind how much sense they made in themselves. None of them did. But after the first month or two he had so much going that there was no question any more of not having something to do. Two hours allotted to work out on the typewriter a critical evaluation of a chapter from one of McAllen's abstruse technical texts. If Barney's mood was sufficiently sour, the evaluation would be unprintable; but it wasn't being printed, and two hours had been disposed of. A day and a half—Earth Standard Time—to construct an operating dam across the stream. He was turning into an experienced landscape architect; the swimming pool in the floor of the valley beneath the cabin might not have been approved by Carstairs of California, but it was the one project out of which he had even drawn some realistic benefit.

Then:

Half an hour to improve his knife-throwing technique.

Fifteen minutes to get the blade of the kitchen knife straightened out afterwards.

Two hours to design a box trap for the capture of one of the fat gray squirrels that always hung about the cabin.

Fifty minutes on a new chess problem. Chess, Barney had discovered, wasn't as hairy as it looked.

Five hours to devise one more completely foolproof method of bringing about the eventual ruin of the association. That made no more practical sense than anything else he was doing—and couldn't, until he knew a great deal more about McAllen's friends than he did now.

But it was considerably more absorbing, say, than even chess.

Brother Chard could beat boredom. He could probably beat another three years of boredom.

He hadn't forgiven anyone for making him do it.

THE END OF YEAR FIVE

For some hours, the association's Altiplano station had been dark and almost deserted. Only the IMT transit lock beneath one of the sprawling ranch houses showed in the vague light spreading out of the big scanning plate in an upper wall section. The plate framed an unimpressive section of the galaxy, a blurred scattering of stars condensing toward the right, and, somewhat left of center, a large misty red globe.

Gone Fishing

John Emanuel Fredericks, seated by himself in one of the two Tube operator chairs, ignored the plate. He was stooped slightly forwards, peering absorbedly through the eyepieces of the operator scanner before him.

Melvin Simms, Psychologist, strolled in presently through the transit lock's door, stopped behind Fredericks, remarked mildly, "Good evening, doctor."

Fredericks started and looked around. "Never heard you arrive, Mel. Where's Ollie?"

"He and Spalding dropped in at Spalding's place in Vermont. They should be along in a few minutes."

"Spalding?" Fredericks repeated inquiringly. "Our revered president intends to observe the results of Ollie's experiment in person?"

"He'll represent the board here," Simms said. "Whereas I, as you may have guessed, represent the outraged psychology department." He nodded at the plate. "That the place?"

"That's it. ET Base Eighteen."

"Not very sharp in the Tube, is it?"

"No. Still plenty of interfering radiation. But it's thinned out enough for contact. Reading 0.19, as of thirty minutes ago." Fredericks indicated the chair beside him. "Sit down if you want a better look."

"Thanks." The psychologist settled himself in the chair, leaned forward and peered into the scanner. After a few seconds he remarked, "Not the most hospitable-looking place—"

Fredericks grunted. "Any of the ecologists will tell you Eighteen's an unspoiled beauty. No problems there—except the ones we bring along ourselves."

Simms grinned faintly. "Well, we're good at doing that, aren't we? Have you looked around for uh ... for McAllen's subject yet?"

"No. Felt Ollie should be present when we find out what's happened. Incidentally, how did the meeting go?"

"You weren't tuned in?" Simms asked, surprised.

"No. Too busy setting things up for contact."

"Well"—Simms sat back in his chair—"I may say it was a regular bear garden for a while, doctor. Psychology expressed itself as being astounded, indignant, offended. In a word, they were hopping mad. I kept out of it, though I admit I was startled when McAllen informed me privately this morning of the five-year project he's been conducting on the quiet. He was accused of crimes ranging ... oh, from the clandestine to the inhumane. And, of course, Ollie was giving it back as good as he got."

"Of course."

"His arguments," Simms went on, pursing his lips reflectively, "were not without merit. That was recognized. Nobody enjoys the idea of euthanasia as a security device. Many of us feel—I do—that it's still preferable to the degree of brain-washing required to produce significant alterations in a personality type of Chard's class."

"Ollie feels that, too," Fredericks said. "The upshot of the original situation, as he saw it, was that Barney Chard had been a dead man from the moment he got on the association's trail. Or a permanently deformed personality."

Simms shook his head. "Not the last. We wouldn't have considered attempting personality alteration in his case."

"Euthanasia then," Fredericks said. "Chard was too intelligent to be thrown off the track, much too unscrupulous to be trusted under any circumstances. So Ollie reported him dead."

The psychologist was silent for some seconds. "The point might be this," he said suddenly. "After my talk with McAllen this morning, I ran an extrapolation on the personality pattern defined for Chard five years ago on the basis of his background. Results indicate he went insane and suicided within a year."

"How reliable are those results?" Fredericks inquired absently.

"No more so than any other indication in individual psychology. But they present a reasonable probability ... and not a very pleasant one."

Fredericks said, "Oliver wasn't unaware of that as a possible outcome. One reason he selected Base Eighteen for the experiment was to make sure he couldn't interfere with the process, once it had begun.

"His feeling, after talking with Chard for some hours, was that Chard was an overcondensed man. That is Oliver's own term, you understand. Chard obviously was intelligent, had a very strong survival drive. He had selected a good personal survival line to follow—good but very narrow. Actually, of course, he was a frightened man. He had been running scared all his life. He couldn't stop."

Simms nodded.

"Base Eighteen stopped him. The things he'd been running from simply no longer existed. Ollie believed Chard would go into a panic when he realized it. The question was what he'd do then. Survival now had a very different aspect. The only dangers threatening him were the ones inherent in the rigid personality structure he had maintained throughout his adult existence. Would he be intelligent enough to understand that? And would his survival urge—with every alternative absolutely barred to him for five years—be strong enough to overcome those dangers?"

"And there," Simms said dryly, "we have two rather large questions." He cleared his throat. "The fact remains, however, that Oliver B. McAllen is a good practical psychologist—as he demonstrated at the meeting."

"I expected Ollie would score on the motions," Fredericks said. "How did that part of it come off?"

"Not too badly. The first motion was passed unanimously. A vote of censure against Dr. McAllen."

Fredericks looked thoughtful. "His seventeenth—I believe?"

"Yes. The fact was mentioned. McAllen admitted he could do no less than vote for this one himself. However, the next motion to receive a majority was, in effect, a generalized agreement that men with such ... ah ... highly specialized skills as Barney Chard's and with comparable intelligence actually would be of great value as members of the association, if it turned out that they could be sufficiently relieved of their more flagrant antisocial tendencies. Considering the qualification, the psychology department could hardly avoid backing that motion. The same with the third one—in effect again that Psychology is to make an unprejudiced study of the results of Dr. McAllen's experiment on Base Eighteen, and report on the desirability of similar experiments when the personality of future subjects appears to warrant them."

"Well," Fredericks said, after a pause, "as far as the association goes, Ollie got what he wanted. As usual." He hesitated. "The other matter—"

"We'll know that shortly." Simms turned his head to listen, added in a lowered voice, "They're coming now."

Dr. Stephen Spalding said to Simms and Fredericks: "Dr. McAllen agrees with me that the man we shall be looking for on Base Eighteen may be dead. If this is indicated, we'll attempt to find some evidence of his death before normal ecological operations on Eighteen are resumed.

"Next, we may find him alive but no longer sane. Dr. Simms and I are both equipped with drug-guns which will then be used to render him insensible. The charge is sufficient to insure he will not wake up again. In this circumstance, caution will be required since he was left on the Base with a loaded gun.

"Third, he may be alive and technically sane, but openly or covertly hostile to us." Spalding glanced briefly at each of the others, then went on, "It is because of this particular possibility that our contact group here has been very carefully selected. If such has been the result of Dr. McAllen's experiment, it will be our disagreeable duty to act as Chard's executioners. To add lifelong confinement or further psychological manipulation to the five solitary years Chard already has spent would be inexcusable.

"Dr. McAllen has told us he did not inform Chard of the actual reason he was being marooned—"

"On the very good grounds," McAllen interrupted, "that if Chard had been told at the outset what the purpose was, he would have preferred killing himself to allowing the purpose to be achieved. Any other human being was Chard's antagonist. It would have been impossible for him to comply with another man's announced intentions."

Simms nodded. "I'll go along on that point, doctor."

Spalding resumed, "It might be a rather immaterial point by now. In any event, Chard's information was that an important 'five-year-plan' of the association made it necessary to restrict him for that length of time. We shall observe him closely. If the indications are that he would act against the association whenever he is given the opportunity, our line will be that the five-year-plan has been concluded, and that he is, therefore, now to be released and will receive adequate compensation for his enforced seclusion. As soon as he is asleep, he will, of course, receive euthanasia. But up to that time, everything must be done to reassure him."

He paused again, concluded, "There is the final possibility that Dr. McAllen's action has had the results he was attempting to bring about.... Ollie, you might speak on that yourself."

McAllen shrugged. "I've already presented my views. Essentially, it's a question of whether Barney Chard was capable of learning that he could live without competing destructively with other human beings. If he has grasped that, he should also be aware by now that Base Eighteen is presently one of the most interesting spots in the known universe."

Simms asked: "Do you expect he'll be grateful for what has occurred?"

"We-e-ll," McAllen said judiciously, turning a little pale, "that, of course, depends on whether he *is* still alive and sane: But if he has survived the five years, I do believe that he will not be dissatisfied with what has happened to him. However"—he shrugged again—"let's get ahead with it. Five years has been a long time to find out whether or not I've murdered a man."

In the momentary silence that followed, he setted himself in the chair Fredericks had vacated, and glanced over at Simms. "You stay seated, Mel," he said. "You represent Psychology here. Use your chair scanner. The plate's still showing no indications of clearing, John?"

"No," said Fredericks. "In another two hours we might have a good picture there. Hardly before."

McAllen said, "We won't wait for it. Simms and I can determine through the scanners approximately what has been going on." He was silent a few seconds; then the blurred red globe in the plate expanded swiftly, filled two thirds of the view space, checked for a moment, then grew once more; finally stopped.

McAllen said irritably, "John, I'm afraid you'll have to take over. My hands don't seem steady enough to handle this properly."

A minute or two passed. The big plate grew increasingly indistinct, all details lost in a muddy wash of orange-brown shades. Green intruded suddenly; then McAllen muttered, "Picking up the cabin now."

There was a moment of silence, then Fredericks cleared his throat. "So far so good, Oliver. We're looking into the cabin. Can't see your man yet—but someone's living here. Eh, Simms?"

"Obviously," the psychologist acknowledged. He hesitated. "And at a guess it's no maniac. The place is in reasonably good order."

"You say Chard isn't in the cabin?" Spalding demanded.

Fredericks said, "Not unless he's deliberately concealing himself. The exit door is open. Hm-m-m. Well, the place isn't entirely deserted, after all."

"What do you mean?" asked Spalding.

"Couple of squirrels sitting in the window," Simms explained.

"In the window? Inside the cabin?"

"Yes," said Fredericks. "Either they strayed in while he was gone, or he's keeping them as pets. Now, should we start looking around outside for Chard?"

"No," Spalding decided. "The Base is too big to attempt to cover at pin-point focus. If he's living in the cabin and has simply gone out, he'll return within a few hours at the most. We'll wait and see what we can deduce from the way he behaves when he shows up." He turned to McAllen. "Ollie," he said, "I think you might allow yourself to relax just a little. This doesn't seem at all bad!"

McAllen grunted. "I don't know," he said. "You're overlooking one thing."

"What's that?"

"I told Chard when to expect us. Unless he's smashed the clock, he knows we're due today. If nothing's wrong—wouldn't he be waiting in the cabin for us?"

Spalding hesitated. "That is a point. He seems to be hiding out. May have prepared an ambush, for that matter. John—"

"Yes?" Fredericks said.

"Step the tubescope down as fine as it will go, and scan that cabin as if you were vacuuming it. There may be some indication—"

"He's already doing that," Simms interrupted.

There was silence again for almost two minutes. Forefinger and thumb of Fredericks' right hand moved with infinite care on a set of dials on the side of the scanner; otherwise neither he nor Simms stirred.

"Oh-hoo-hoo-HAW!" Dr. John Fredericks cried suddenly. "Oh-hoo-hoo-HAW! A message, Ollie! Your Mr. Chard has left you a ... hoo-hoo ... message."

For a moment McAllen couldn't see clearly through the scanner. Fredericks was still laughing; Simms was saying in a rapid voice, "It's quite all right, doctor! Quite all right. Your man's sane, quite sane. In fact you've made, one might guess, a one hundred per cent convert to the McAllen approach to life. Can't you *see* it?"

"No," gasped McAllen. He had a vague impression of the top of the desk in the main room of the cabin, of something white—a white card—taped to it, of blurred printing on the card. "Nothing's getting *that* boy unduly excited any more," Simms' voice went on beside him. "Not even the prospect of seeing visitors from Earth for the first time in five years. But he's letting you know it's perfectly all right to make yourself at home in his cabin until he gets back. Here, let me—"

He reached past McAllen, adjusted the scanner. The printing on the card swam suddenly into focus before McAllen's eyes.

The message was terse, self-explanatory, to the point:

GONE FISHING,

Regards,
B. Chard.